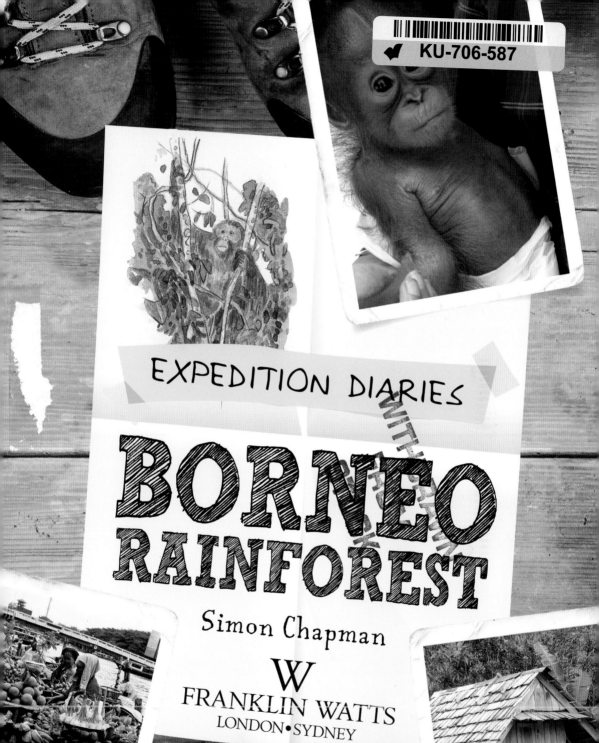

EXPEDITION DIARIES

BORNEO RAINFOREST

Simon Chapman

W
FRANKLIN WATTS
LONDON · SYDNEY

Expedition to the Borneo Rainforest

I'm going to the island of Borneo in South-east Asia. My plan is to look for orangutans, gibbons and monkeys in the rainforest there.

My point of arrival in Borneo is the town of Banjarmasin, in the far south of the island. Banjarmasin is a bit like the city of Venice in Italy, as there are so many canals that the way you get around is by boat, not car.

Personal kit
- Canvas-top jungle boots, with gaiters to keep the leeches out
- Lightweight long-sleeved shirt and trousers (to stop leeches again!)
- Rucksack, lightweight sleeping bag and mosquito net
- Insect repellent gel, so I can smear it round the tops of my boots to discourage leeches
- Torch (waterproof) and compass
- Rain cape
- Medical kit, with malaria tablets, antiseptic and fungal powder

To buy in Borneo
- Parang (bush knife), sleeping mat, cooking pot

PAPERWORK!
I'll also need to organise a Surat Jalan. (It means 'permission to walk'). This permit will let me travel in Kutai National Park and in the Apo Kayan mountain rainforest.

BORNEO

Borneo is the third largest island in the world, and is divided between Indonesia, Malaysia and Brunei. The Sarawak and Sabah provinces on the northwest coast of the island belong to Malaysia, while the rest of the island provinces of Central, North, East, South and West Kalimantan belong to Indonesia. The island is largely mountainous with lowland areas predominantly in Central Kalimantan and Sarawak.

Rivers form the main transport networks, but some rivers in the north are hard to navigate, making the northern interior of Borneo relatively unexploited. The hot and humid climate of Borneo ensures that the island is one of the most biodiverse places in the world, with the Bornean clouded leopard, proboscis monkeys and orangutans among its inhabitants.

Borneo

Fly into Syamsudin Noor Airport in Banjarmasin

TRAVEL PLANNING

I'll be travelling deep into the lowland rainforest and mangrove swamps of Kutai National Park on the east coast of Kalimantan. Getting there has needed a lot of planning. Very few people there will speak English so I have used books and the Internet to teach myself enough Indonesian to be able to get a boat ride and the permits that I will need.

Diseases

The mosquitoes in Kalimantan carry malaria, so I'll need to take antimalarial tablets to kill off any parasites that get into my blood. Also, most of the drinking water will come straight from the rivers. I'll need special chlorine tablets to kill germs in the water and, before I set off, I'll need injections against water-borne diseases, like cholera and typhoid.

BRUNEI

South China Sea

SARAWAK
(MALAYSIA)

SABAH
(MALAYSIA)

Long Uro

Long
Sungai
Barang

RIVER KAYAN

Mentoko

RIVER KAPUAS

Long
Ampung

Kutai
National
Park

Sangatta

Teluk
Kaba

KALIMANTAN
(INDONESIA)

RIVER MAHAKAM

RIVER BARITO

Bontang

Banjarmasin

Samarinda

Java Sea

KUTAI NATIONAL PARK

Kutai National Park is an area of
tropical rainforest, with some mangrove
swamps and freshwater lakes. Tropical
rainforests like this grow in warm, humid
places and typically receive anywhere
between 2 to 6 metres of rainfall each
year. The park is 2,000 square kilometres
in size, but fire, logging and mining
have threatened to reduce the park area,
despite its protected status. The park is
home to ten species of primate, including
orangutans, 90 species of mammal, 300
species of bird and 958 species of plant.

Banjarmasin

One plane, two minibuses and two motorbike taxi rides to get here, but I'm now in Kalimantan, the Indonesian part of Borneo.

I was feeling quite pleased, until I just locked myself out of my room.

Now feeling hot and tired ...

I have been 'adopted' by a student called Nuryaddin, who wants to practise his English. I'm staying at his father's stilt house (left) on a channel of the Barito river for a couple of nights.

View across the river from Nuryaddin's house.

We hired a 9-metre long motor boat, called a klotok, for a trip to a floating market on the Barito river.

Life here revolves around the river; it's a transport route and home.

To get to the market we motored through a back alley canal, lined by houses on stilts over the water, with others built on floating logs.

There are kids here swimming next to people having their early morning wash, or washing their clothes. Later, I washed myself in the river. I also had a poo in it, which sounds gross, but everyone does it.

LATER...

Went to a little forested island where we were swarmed over by long-tailed macaque monkeys as we fed them peanuts. A big male decided to climb up me to grab the packet.

There is a Brahminy kite circling overhead.

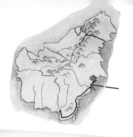

Samarinda

9 SEP, late at night, in a bus on a mud road

All the rainforest near to Banjarmasin has been cut down for logging or palm oil plantations, so I'm on a bus to Samarinda, which is further up the coast.

From Samarinda I will go to Kutai National Park (where there is coastal rainforest). I haven't seen any primary rainforest yet – it's all secondary regrowth, scrub or tall 'alang-alang' grass.

PALM OIL PLANTATIONS

Palm oil is a vegetable oil, and the palm oil trees grow in plantations in tropical climates, like Borneo's. Often, rainforest is chopped down for these plantations, destroying animal habitats and a variety of plant species. It is estimated that 1,000 to 5,000 orangutans are killed every year because of palm oil development.

The scenery coming into Samarinda shows what an area looks like after deforestation, with dead, white trunks surrounded by lush scrub vegetation and blackened stumps on

burnt red earth.

I'm getting a longboat to the far side of Kutai National Park with two researchers, Liz and Ali, from New Zealand.

Mosque in Samarinda opposite the hotel.

We'll be staying at a disused research station called Mentoko for several days. Mentoko is basically an abandoned house deep in the rainforest. We've been organising boat times and prices, and getting letters of permission to go into the national park.

Hopefully, I'll be in the rainforest tomorrow evening.

Bought a new parang. I feel like a proper jungle explorer now.

LATER...

Departure time was 1.00 PM, then 3.00 PM then 4.30 PM. Finally set off at 6.00 PM. Tammy Wynette's song 'Stand By Your Man' is wailing out of a loudspeaker.

Mentoko

We're heading up the coast, passed nipa palm (Nypa fruticans) forests, and now we're hitting cultivated country; first just the odd hut, now villages with lots of coconut and banana palms.

Most of last night was pretty bad. I felt ill, and the thumping vibration of the long boat engine meant sleep was impossible.

Arrived at Sangatta, where my Indonesian came in very handy for convincing the officials that our permits were OK. In the National Park office there was a very clingy baby orangutan, called Johnny, that tried to drink my cup of tea. Loggers had killed his mother, but kept the baby to sell.

The park guards rescued him.

They hope that when Johnny is older he will live wild in the forest again (although this might never happen as he is already too used to humans).

10

We are now heading upriver in an overloaded 'ketinting' (a small wooden canoe with an outboard motor – named after the noise it makes).

One-metre long monitor lizards scuttle up the banks as we pass.

I've also spotted troupes of macaque monkeys.

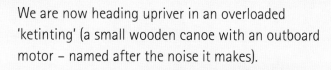

At one set of rapids we had to go on foot for a short while. It was tough machete work, hacking through the dense vegetation on the riverbank.

12 SEP

This is real jungle explorer stuff! We're at the disused hut, now set up with mosquito net and tarpaulin.

Dinner of stewed vegetables and rice is boiling in billy cans over a small wood fire. Outside there are buzzes, clicks and whirrs all around the hut, and fireflies and big moths whose eyes glow in the firelight.

There is also something that **barks like a small dog,** rustling around the back of the hut. Luckily, the smoke from the fire seems to be keeping the mosquitoes away.

This gecko (Gekko gecko) was making the barking noise.

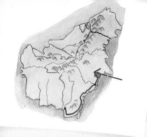

Leech Attack!

I'm lying under my mosquito net in the disused research hut. Behind us there is a loud dawn chorus of Müller's Bornean gibbons (*Hylobates muelleri*) calling:

'Owa Owa Owawawawawa'

GIBBONS

Gibbons are small apes found in tropical rainforest biomes in Southeast Asia. They have a distinctive call – loud and musical – which carries over long distances. Gibbons swing from tree to tree using their long arms, and they rarely visit the forest floor. They feed on fruit, leaves and insects.

12

I HATE leeches!

I just rolled down my sock and there they were, waving their leechy little snouts, saying 'so long and thanks for the blood!' I've just found the third one today –

Yeurrk!

Palm in shrub layer. Very quick sketch as it started to rain again and I was getting leeched badly.

Leeches. I don't need to burn them off. I'm so insensitive that they fill up with blood (my blood!) before I notice.

I know leeches do very little harm, but when a full one rolls out, it really makes your skin crawl. There was a circular spot of blood on my ankle. I treated it with antiseptic, but half an hour later it was still oozing blood (leeches have 'anti-coagulant' spit).

13

Orangutan Sighting

I've just seen an orangutan!

It was quite close – only about 100 metres from the hut – across a clearing, sitting at the foot of some thin trees.

A butterfly that I trapped in my map case.

ORANGUTAN (PONGO PYGMAEUS AND PONGO ABELII)

Orangutans live in the lowland forests of Borneo and Sumatra. They use their long, powerful arms to move around in the trees. They eat wild fruits, such as figs and lychees, and are key to the dispersal of seeds throughout the forest. The destruction of the orangutans' forest habitat means they are considered to be endangered.

The orangutan watched us, then lazily climbed the nearest tree, bending the thin trunk over with its weight and making it easy to follow. Altogether we must have watched him for ten or fifteen minutes, but it seemed like hours.

14

We caught glimpses of the orangutan later, along with stick insects, flying squirrels and rhinoceros hornbills (right). We heard many more hornbills. They can be heard from a long distance when they fly as they have sound-amplifying air sacs in their wings.

Preparing to head out on a trek wth Liz and Ali.

Every trip into the forest is like preparing for a mini expedition: fungal powder, gaiters covered in jungle gel, more jungle gel covering exposed skin, pouch containing camera, more repellent for leech removal, a compass and, of course, my trusty *parang*.

In the forest the air is still and so humid. You have to drink because you are losing so much fluid.

You pour sweat and get smelly very quickly.

Pitcher plant. The insect trapping cup comes from an extension of the central spine of the leaf.

15

Lost

14 SEP, 2.30 PM

I'm just back from a trek. We cut notches on tree trunks so we wouldn't get lost,

but managed to get lost anyway ...

which was quite frightening, and not very clever. We didn't spot any wildlife – we were too noisy (and the jungle was too thick). But by walking slowly or staying still you see more animals. When you stop, gradually all the noises return after the disturbance you have caused – first the insects, then the birds – maybe a woodpecker or some twittering in the canopy.

Suddenly,

you'll hear a dry clatter and you'll look round hoping it's a monkey or some other animal, but it's usually just a large dead leaf or a falling branch.

Looking up at the trunk of a strangler fig. It's hard to tell if the original tree is still under there or has rotted away.

Eventually, we followed the sound of rushing water, got to the river and followed it back to the hut.

After the intense humidity of the forest, swimming in the river and sunbathing on the beach was bliss, until I was discovered by sweat bees.

These little black bees kept landing on the places where I am sweating the most, tickling my skin with their mouthparts as they try to lick up the salt. Shaking them off doesn't get rid of them and brushing them off was no good, as I have just discovered, because they sting you. **Ouch!**

LATER...

Fascinated by this pill millipede. It curls up into a perfect ball when disturbed, and has an amazing robot-like quality. It trundles to the table's edge, then turns off at an angle until it comes to the next edge.

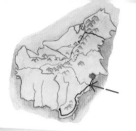

Teluk Kaba

We're heading off to journey out to Teluk Kaba, a coastal part of Kutai National Park where there are meant to be big-nosed proboscis monkeys (Nasalis larvatus, left) in the mangroves.

On the way back down from Mentoko to Teluk Kaba, I saw some huge, amazingly beautiful stork-billed kingfishers. They were bright orange, about 30 cm long, with bright red beaks and shiny turquoise wings.

A stork-billed kingfisher (Pelargopsis capensis).

It took about three hours to get back to Sangatta, passing through several small rapids.

I've just pigged out as if I hadn't eaten for a week!

I had chicken noodle soup, fried chicken, two cups of tea and three doughnuts – and regained my strength virtually immediately.

I have hired another boat, together with Liz and Ali, to head round the coast to Teluk Kaba where there are mangrove swamps.

The sea must be very shallow here, as there are quite a few of these fishing shacks on stilts, as well as plaited palm fish traps (channels to divert schools of fish into).

Teluk Kaba, after dark

The boat dropped us off in waist-high water, 20 m from the shore.

I waded to land to meet a reception committee consisting of a small, eager young man, who shook our hands excitedly, and a disinterested-looking orangutan that apparently lives here.

LATER...

Almost walked straight past a tarsier (Cephalopachus bancanus) in a tree - well, it was dark!

Mangrove Swamp

So hot today!

Well over 30 degrees Celsius

I'll need the litres of water I've brought with me.

It's also incredibly humid (at least 80 per cent) and the mosquitoes are bad. I don't feel like doing anything, but we walk down to the natural harbour on the river to look at the mangroves there.

MANGROVE TREES

Mangrove trees are found in forests along sheltered coasts of Borneo, where they grow in the saline (salty) soil. They have adapted to the harsh environment, with tough roots to withstand tidal changes and special bark and leaves to cope with the salty conditions. These forests are an important habitat for fish, crabs, and prawns, and they help protect coastlines from tidal erosion.

It's hard to get off the few paths as it's all mangrove forest. Each time I set off, I come to shallow lakes or swampy areas with lots of birds, but I can't get to the edge because of the mangroves.

When I try to push my way through I send egrets and herons squawking on their way every few steps. I started wading into what I thought was mud, but then I realised it was basically masses of guano –

bird poo – and it
STANK!

Hundreds of crabs scurried across the surface, running down holes and sealing themselves in whenever danger (i.e. me) came near. Beyond, I could see pools where mudskippers were fighting (above). They look like relics from dinosaur times!

LATER...

I just saw a small leopard cat prowling under the bushes. So that's what the birds are so scared of!

Bird Roost

16 SEP, 5.00 PM

The egrets, herons and cormorants are coming in to roost for the night. It's really spectacular to watch.

Squadron after squadron coming in to land, and swooping really close to my head.

There are hunch-necked night herons that croak 'quark' as they fly, and flocks of black ibis.

The anhingas, or 'snake birds' (above), are the strangest of all; with their crooked necks and thin heads that don't seem to fit on the rest of the bird.

By sundown whole sections of forest were white with egrets. With no warning, they would suddenly fly up, filling the air like confetti, before landing all together in another group of trees.

Their SQUAWKING!
continued until well after dark.

Tonight, the clattering frog noise is like a parade ground of troops fumbling with their rifles as they go through drill, and is easily drowning out the feeble attempts of the crickets chirping.

17 SEP

It's been raining this morning like I've never seen it rain before!

Stuck inside, we were trying to wash down a meal of coconut scrapings, peanuts and rice with sweet tea in the smoky cooking hut.

Then we heard a creaking noise and a thud on the door. It sounded like creepy horror-movie sound effects ...

It turned out to be the orangutan that lives semi-wild near here. It comes to the hut where it knows it will find food. It saw the peanuts I was holding and climbed up me – locking its legs around my waist. It only got off when Ali threw more peanuts off the veranda!

23

Forest Hike

When it stopped raining we went for a hike to look for proboscis monkeys.

We followed a logging track through bushy secondary growth forest. Some of the primary rainforest was destroyed by big fires a few years ago. Other areas have been cut down by loggers.

The best forest area – people tell us – is the Apo Kayan in the centre of Borneo. Here the rivers are too small to transport lumber, so the trees haven't been cut down.

PROBOSCIS MONKEY (NASALIS LARVATUS)

Proboscis monkeys are found in the forests of Borneo, close to rivers, coasts and swamps. They spend most of their time in the trees and swimming in the nearby waters. Males use their distinctive nose as an echo chamber when they call to attract a mate. Unfortunately, these monkeys are under threat because of forest clearance.

I've seen two wild pigs and a couple of sambar deer (left),

but no monkeys.

Later on we saw the deer really close to the house. They let us feed them papaya leaves. We had papaya leaves ourselves today. They are disgustingly bitter, but apparently have anti-malarial properties.

Evening at the hut

A scrape on my knee has gone septic.

I just pressed the scab and loads of pus came out. It went manky when I washed it yesterday, and I'm cursing myself for not smearing it with loads of antiseptic and putting on a wound dressing.

The daily 6 PM flypast of local fruit bats.

LATER...

The hut got visited again by the orangutan who (we think) stole a medical kit as it had cotton buds sticking out of its mouth!

25

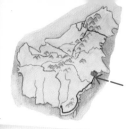

Sangkima River

It's early morning, and today we're heading deeper inland on the river to where the rainforest is less disturbed.

It's here that we'll have the best chance to see monkeys.

Midday, Sangkima river

The Sangkima river is the smallest river I've been on yet.

We had to wait for the tide to rise before entering the narrow mangrove and nipa palm-lined channel. The rainforest trees are so close that we can reach out and touch the leaves as we pass.

Wow!
A kingfisher just sped past.

A coucal cuckoo (*Centropus sinensis*, right) is shrieking from a riverside tree. Up on bendy branches, common long-tailed, or crab-eating, macaques (*Macaca fascicularis*, left) are watching us.

26

In the trees overhead we can see proboscis monkeys moving around.

As we get closer, we can see there are about 15 individuals – perhaps two families – looking down at us. They really are unique-looking animals, with their distinctive fat-bellies and oversized noses (the males have the larger ones!).

Approaching sunset

After less than an hour we turned around and headed back to the sea. The Sun was starting to go down. My thoughts turn towards tomorrow. I'm heading back to Samarinda, before flying to Apo Kayan where I'll be staying in a Kenyah Dayak village.

APO KAYAN

The Apo Kayan is a remote, highland region of Borneo where the Kayan river flows. The thick forest of this plateau lies close to the Malaysian border in East Kalimantan, Indonesia, and is a favourite jungle trekking area for visitors. Tourists also come to the area to observe the life and traditional culture of the native Kenyah Dayak people who live in Apo Kayan.

Buzzing About

We got up at 4.30 AM for the speedboat back to Samarinda.

It was pure hell!

I've never gone through such torture as the two-hour speed boat ride in rough seas. With every wave we hit, I was thrown up into the air to land with a spine-jarring thud.

The driver even put his safety helmet on it was so rough!

20 SEP

I buzzed around Samarinda in high spirits all day, even though my Mentoko expedition party is splitting up.

We're heading to various parts of Indonesia, and I'm teaming up with two environmentalists from Australia and the USA to go to Apo Kayan; the big tribal area in the middle of Borneo.

I'm sitting in a local café after buying a durian: a very smelly fruit that

people SAY is delicious, but it's

yuck!

The custard-like mush inside is the same colour as the pus from my knee – and almost as disgusting. Durian smells of onion, mixed with cleaning fluid; it's sweet – though a bit sickly – with an oniony aftertaste. Tigers and orangutans in Sumatra are said to feast on fallen durians. The sugars in the fruit ferment into alcohol and the animals get drunk!

7.15 PM and I'm still **burping** up durian aftertaste.

21 SEP, Samarinda airport

Spent yesterday afternoon buying gifts for the Kenyah Dayak tribe I'll be staying with.

I also bought some blankets and canned food.

LATER...

Coming in to land in Apo Kayan after an amazing flight.

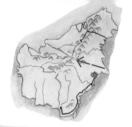

Apo Kayan

I've just woken up after a cold night on the hard floor of a longhouse.

Around me people are busy: winnowing, sieving, pounding rice. Chickens are squawking and cockerels are crowing. I can hear pigs on the ground beneath the longhouse, snuffling up the food scraps.

The flight here yesterday in a little Twin Otter aircraft was spectacular.

Rice barn at Long Uro.

We flew over burnt forest and logged forest, then finally got to the mountains of the Apo Kayan, which is covered with dense primary rainforest. A strip of light green grass showed us where a clearing had been cut for a runway.

It felt as though I'd finally arrived in the rainforest.

30

Soon, we were walking on a slippery log-covered trail by the Kayan River towards Long Uro, with a group returning to their village.

KENYAH DAYAK

The Kenyah Dayak people live in isolated villages across Sarawak, Malaysia, and North and East Kalimantan. Traditionally, Kenyah Dayak people farmed rice in jungle clearings. A village often consists of one or two large communal houses, with rooms at the back and a covered veranda.

The village of Long Uro has a couple of 50-m longhouses on poles, set about 1-and-a-half metres above the ground. I'm sitting in one of these right now. My travelling companions are staying in their own tent.

Everywhere there are designs like these. This one was painted on the sides of a longhouse. The pictures of tigers puzzle me though, as there have never been tigers on Borneo. Perhaps they are meant to be 'clouded leopards', which do live here.

LATER...

I'm moving further upstream tomorrow from where I'll be heading deep into the rainforest.

Long Sungai Barang

It seems as though I'm the last one to wake up again.

There are the usual noises, but also some Indonesian country and western-type music blaring out of one of the nearby houses.

I'm staying in Long Sungai Barang, near the headwaters of the Kayan river.

It's a village of wooden plank huts, a couple of longhouses and some brightly painted rice barns. I'm staying with the headman (Ubang) and his wife (Pelagit) who are kind, and keep bringing lots of food and blankets.

My Indonesian is getting pretty good (I think!). I'm doing a lot of haggling over prices for guides to take me into the rainforest. I'm planning to head up into the mountains with a hunting party in the next day or two.

Kenyah Dayak woman giggling at my Indonesian.

KAYAN MENTARANG NATIONAL PARK

This park in Kalimantan covers 13,605 km – the largest protected area of rainforest in Borneo. The park contains a variety of biomes including lowland forests, highland forests and even some savannah. At least 150 mammals (including the clouded leopard) and 300 species of bird live there.

If we're lucky we might even find tracks of the secretive clouded leopard. I'm only about 50 km away from the edge of the Kayan Mentarang National Park.

The hunters use sumpits. These are two-metre long blowpipes that are 'rifled' in a spiral inside the tube to stabilise the blow dart. The spear tip on the end is for hunting pigs.

The killing end of a sumpit (blowpipe).

LATER...

It starts to rain heavily just after lunch, and doesn't stop all afternoon.

Thunderstorms

It's pouring with rain - again - and I'm stuck here until the weather eases.

I've done lots of sketching though, which has been a real talking point for the villagers who tell me the names of the birds and animals I am drawing.

Kenyah girls pounding rice.

I was taken on a walk around some flooded fields. Some were overgrown with metre-high 'alang-alang' spear grass (left). It has sharp, serrated edges.

You can cut yourself as you try to push through it ...
as I found out.

Then rumbles of thunder started, so we had to head back. It's getting cooler now. It's amazing how cold it gets at night. I really need the blankets (I'm also sleeping fully clothed!).

KAYAN RIVER

Rising in the interior mountains between Sarawak, Malaysia and North Kalimantan, the Kayan river flows through North Kalimantan before splitting into three branches and several cross channels forming a delta, which flows into the Celebes Sea. Freshwater dolphins can be found in its waters.

The weather has finally cleared, but it's rained a lot overnight. The nearby Kayan river has risen 50 cm, so we have to be cautious for flood surges when washing. Arrangements are simple:

Kenyah woman with baby in carrier.

you wash upstream, and anywhere below ten metres downstream is the toilet.

Design on a rice barn.

Food is entirely based on what is caught or grown nearby; so lots of white rice and greens – 'jungle greens' – which can be anything from stewed papaya leaves to stewed ferns. Also, there's pork and deer meat, and lots of pineapple and crispy bits of rice flour batter – **delicious!**

Into the Rainforest

I'm in the forest with Ubang, on our way to meet up with a friend of his who lives further up the hillside.

Loving this!

We're wading through fast flowing rivers and hacking out a path through thickets (right). While I use my heavy *parang*, Ubang uses a thin sword-like knife called a *mandau*. This is a headhunting blade.

The Kenyah Dayak people used to cut off the heads of their enemies. I haven't seen any skulls hanging up at any of the Kenyah Dayak longhouses –

to be honest I'm relieved!

A bromeliad growing on tree fern.

36

BINTURONG (ARCTICTIS BINTURONG)

The binturong is a omnivorous mammal found in the forests of Southeast Asia. They share characteristics with mongooses and genets. They have dark, shaggy fur, a snout and a long, furry tail, which they use to help with balance and grip. Binturong eat fruit, insects, birds and rodents.

Afternoon rest

I've just seen a troupe of langur monkeys through the trees.

These were the first animals I've seen here, though we heard gibbons and binturongs, which make a weird wailing sound.

It's only when I grab a rest from the gruelling walking pace that the full wonder of this place becomes apparent. It's cooler now than earlier, and everything is soaked from the rain. There isn't a continuous canopy as such; just lots of tall trees covered in climbers and bromeliads – and lower down lots of palms and tree ferns.

I can hear all sorts of

clicks, whirrs and hammering sounds,

but only ever get glimpses of the odd warbler-like bird. Of course as soon as I stop, I get swarmed by mosquitoes, and leeches (I have flicked at least a hundred off my boots).

Mountain Retreat

I'm sitting in an empty rice barn on stilts, on a deforested hillside. I'm sharing a meal of jungle greens and heaps of sticky rice, livened up with my two reserve cans of sardines.

We've stopped just short of a mountain, which we're going to set off early to climb, then loop round back to Long Sungai Barang over the next couple of days.

I'm sitting outside the rice barn now. It's cold outside and mist is rolling down over the forested hills around me. I'm watching as a seemingly endless stream of bats fly out of a cave up in a limestone cliff face.

Bats streaming out of cave.

A bat hawk (*Macheiramphus alcinus*) is **buzzing** the bats as it attempts to catch one in mid-air.

BAT HAWK

Bat hawks are birds of prey that live and hunt in tropical forests and some grasslands. In Borneo they hunt near limestone caves where their favourite prey – bats – are often found. When the bats emerge at dusk, bat hawks swoop down, capture and swallow each bat whole in mid-air.

A muntjac deer paused at the edge of the cleared forest, before disappearing back into the shadows. There are noises all around – a stream bubbling in the valley, the voices of Dayak youths in the rice barn behind me, overlaid by crickets, cicadas and some distant birdsong.

26 SEP, 6 AM

Ubang and I set off early, walking up and up through the forest for a couple of hours.

The pace is fast, and it has put us nearly at the top, where paths branch off for Long Sungai Barang and another village called Mahak Baru.

Waterfall Accident

It's easy to get caught up in the magical qualities of the rainforest, and here you really get an idea of the primary forest that once completely covered Borneo.

LOWLAND RAINFOREST

The lowland rainforests of Borneo experience a warm, moist climate which is an ideal place for 10,000 species of different plants to grow. Here, in the montane/sub-montane forest conditions, trees grow thinner than the trees I saw at Kutai, and there are more tree ferns covered with moss and dotted with bromeliads.

The trees are low – making it atmospheric – with branches covered in thick, damp moss.

I have to remember to watch out for snakes.

The terrain is very tricky. I am constantly up to my ankles in muck. Trying to climb over entwined roots is made even more difficult because they can suddenly part, trapping my feet.

We keep going up, but each time I think we have reached the top, it proves only to be another false summit, and the path continues on.

I'm taking a break after having a close call with a waterfall – much to Ubang's frustration.

We were picking our way down alongside a very fast flowing stream.

Ubang got further and further ahead, while I was getting tired and sliding on slimy rocks almost every step. I think I was trying to catch up when I fell right over a small waterfall, landing heavily on my hands and my left knee. Luckily, I haven't done any serious damage – although my knee is swelling up. I've put some cold water from the stream on it while I rest here.

LATER...

This spider, with a 3 cm-wide shell on its back and a web that stretched several metres between two trees, caught a 6 cm-long hornet as I drew this.

Forest Hunt

We veered away from the river, and headed up and along through some dense forest.

Ubang said this is the area where clouded leopards live. Later, I saw something cat-like cross ahead of us – although I think it was a palm civet.

Ubang called it 'binatang', which simply means 'beast'.

Palm civet (Paradoxurus hermaphroditus) up a tree at night.

12 PM

We left the forest and rose up again through worked and unworked fields, until we reached a bumpy grass airstrip.

Ubang met a friend and we hiked to the guy's hut, where we are now. He has a rifle and a small dog, and says he will come with us on our trek back to Long Sungai Barang tomorrow.

Its 7 PM and **I'm feeling exhausted** and my **knee is sore**.

It's cold and uncomfortable on the floor of the hut now they've put the fire out. Perhaps I should have slept upstairs with the others, but I wanted to stay with my gear.

My rucksack is full of cockroaches this morning. I also found several in my pants! **Yeuw!**

27 SEP, 12 PM

We've just killed a deer.

Ubang's friend's dog was barking up ahead, and both men ran off. I heard a gun shot and saw Ubang hack at something with his mandau. There was a loud splash and I could see a sambar deer lying in the stream. I helped pull the carcass onto the shore. Ubang built a fire, while his friend skinned the carcass and started butchering it. Before long we were eating deer meat and deer heart with rice for lunch.

I gave this pit viper we saw later a wide berth!

Final Leg

28 SEP, Long Sungai Barang

Humped it back to Long Sungai Barang where it was good to get fed and fussed over.

Heading down river to Long Uro tomorrow.

29 SEP, back at Long Uro

The heat and humidity has totally sapped any energy I had. I drew this blue-winged pitta (left).

1 OCT, Long Ampung Airstrip

It was supposed to be a lazy day preparing for the flight to Banjarmasin.

Except when I was crossing a log bridge in the rain, I slipped, my bad knee gave out and I fell off! I'm surprised that I only have slight bruises and grazes.

Woke up this morning to find my bed **mattress on FIRE!**

The room was filled with smoke and an Australian woman from the room next door was coughing her guts out trying to wake me. I was really dazed.

Two guys from the hotel barged in and shouted something which I didn't understand and threw buckets of water over the bed.

I pushed some money into their hands, said goodbye and in minutes was on the street hailing a guy on a motorcycle to take me to the airstrip for a plane, which I got to with only half an hour to spare.

Now I'm back in Jakarta — Borneo seems a long way away.

And it's only now that I've realised what must have happened at the hotel. I got back there at about 4 AM and it was locked up. So I climbed up to get in via the balcony. Before going to sleep I lit some mosquito coils (right). They obviously fell onto the bed and set fire to the mattress.

Very dangerous — I won't make that mistake again.

45

6 October, Singapore

I'm staying in an air-conditioned, high-rise tower block that seems about a million miles from the Borneo rainforest, though I'm not really that far away.

Getting right into the heart of Kutai National Park was amazing, but I could never have expected to see an orangutan on my first day there. Those leech-ridden forests are beautiful and incredibly biodiverse, but they are also disappearing fast under the threat of logging and farming. I really hope they can be saved.

Right now I'm off to the police station - to pick up the two metre-long Dayak blowpipe I bought in Samarinda, when I got back from the Apo Kayan. I suppose I shouldn't have been surprised when the customs men took it from me when I landed here. But I am pleased they are giving it back. It's going to be a great souvenir from a fantastic trip!